CEZANNE

Cezanne

with an introduction by Basil Taylor

MARBORO BOOKS · NEW YORK

ACKNOWLEDGMENTS

The paintings in this volume are reproduced by kind permission of the following collections and galleries to which they belong: The Louvre, Paris (Plates i, v, vi, viii, xv, xvi, xix, xx, xxi, xxiv, xxix, xxxviii, xlv); The Courtauld Institute, London (Plates xxiii, xxvi, xxx, xxxii, xxxiii, xxxix, xlii); The Trustees of the Tate Gallery, London (Plates xi, xxvii, xxxiv, xlviii); The National Gallery, London (Plate xliii); The Museum of Art, Sao Paulo (Plates xvii, xxxi); The Petit Palais Museum, Paris (Plate xliv); The National Gallery, Prague (Plates xxii, xl); The Art Institute, Chicago (Plates vii, xxxvii); The Museum of Art, Philadelphia (Plates xlvi, xlvii); The Guggenheim Museum, New York (Plate xli); The Lord Rothschild Collection, Cambridge (Plates ix, xxviii); The Lehman Collection, New York (Plate xxv); The Renand Collection, Paris (Plate iii); The Bührle Collection, Zurich (Plates xiv, xxxvi); The Niarchos Collection (Plate iv). The paintings reproduced on Plates ii, x, xii, xiii, xviii, xxxv are in private collections. The paintings reproduced on Plates i—iii, v—viii, x, xii—xxi, xxiv—xxvi, xxix, xxxi—xxxiii, xxxv, xxxvi, xxxviii, xxxix, xli, xliv, xlv, xlvii were photographed by Photographie Giraudon, Paris. The frontispiece is reproduced by courtesy of The Art Institute of Chicago.

Published by

MARBORO BOOKS

131 Varick Street · New York, 13, N.Y.

By arrangement with

Books for Pleasure Ltd., London

© Books for Pleasure Ltd. 1961

Printed in Czechoslovakia

T 695

Contents

Introduction

CÉZANNE has been the patron-hero of painting for at least the first forty years of our century, and while his works have had the same kind of status in the history of art as Masaccio's frescoes in the Brancacci Chapel or the Sistine ceiling, it is perhaps the power of his presence and the virility of his ideals, more than the example of any single picture, which has inspired even artists whose intention and practice have been quite different from his own. Although his influence was to be posthumous and in spite of his personal detachment for so many years from the life of his time, he belonged most intimately to the revolutionary current in nineteenth-century art.

Except for a few pictures of allegorical or imaginative subjects made in his twenties, he based his art upon the commonest features of ordinary life, or the elemental themes of European painting, the human head and figure, the nude, fruit, flowers, household properties and landscape, above all the Provençal landscape, which was not to be considered picturesque until he had transformed its harsh features into a series of glowing modern icons and joined it to the Campagna or the flat waterways of Holland as one of the fundamental landscapes of art. In the last thirty-five years of his life his painting was founded upon a direct visual perception of things; he would have agreed with Courbet that 'the art of painting can only consist of the representation of objects visible and tangible to the painter'. And at the heart of his exceptional integrity was a purity of perception which, although it resulted in works of an unprecedented character, showed nevertheless the typical Romantic sincerity of the nineteenth century, of a Constable, for example, or a Corot or a Monet.

At this time when a devotion to the analysis of colour perception and of the relationship between light and colour was as dominant as the study of space and proportion had been in fifteenth-century Italy, he attempted to create a new chromatic art in which the natural colour of the visible world in all its radiance, of apples or trees or sky, was to be brought into harmony with the ideal colour of a pictorial design determined by the necessities of structural firmness and order. His mature paintings were to have an unexampled intensity, every touch of pigment upon their surface not only being informed by his intense visual experience but contributing directly to the vitality and coherence of the whole work. If many non-figurative painters in the 1960's would regard as old-fashioned such planned and premeditated works, organisms growing gradually by sketch, trial and constant deliberation towards completeness, they would at least respect Cézanne's devotion to the significance of the individual brush stroke as being the essential constituent of his art, not just the artist's own property, in a special sense, but the very embodiment of his understanding and sensations.

But if the formal and physical characteristics of his painting are in these ways so characteristic of the most radical ideas of his time and so significant for the period to follow, it has been the uncompromising nature of his personality and the conduct of his creative life which has given him a unique status. He was the most remarkable example in his age of a self-made painter, one not presented with facility and technical confidence from the beginning, like a Millais or a Meissonier, but a man who had painfully to uncover his talent and find the means to give shape to his ideals. With a Cartesian rigour, motivated by humility rather than scepticism, he had to fight his way back to the very elements of visual sensation and pictorial method.

His life shows an obstinate and fierce passion working within an unromantic, bourgeois shell. With his lifelong struggle with the realities of nature went an enduring sense of contest with society and its grappling conventions and opinions. A dogged modesty about his powers and the progress of his painting was mingled with a proud awareness of his own self-sufficiency. Nothing but the secure and eternal values of art could be taken for granted; every step had to be tested by personal experience and in action upon the canvas. And from this ideal emerged another aspect of his sincerity, a patience and slowness which is the quality distinguishing his work most obviously from the excited improvisations of our own time. As a man of impulsive behaviour, he reserved all that patience which could not be spared for his domestic and social life for the understanding of his sensations and the unfolding of his art. When he punished a canvas with a brush or a knife or threw it out of the window, that was because his powers had, in his view, failed or deserted him.

To these qualities must be added his attitude to material success and fame. Gauguin's ruthless withdrawal from modern civilisation, or the worldly failure of Van Gogh and the destruction of his physical and mental being, have seemed more arresting to the public, but they have never aroused the sympathy and respect of artists so strongly as Cézanne's less dramatic combat with art and nature.

Paul Cézanne was born at Aix-en-Provence in January 1839, his family having settled there in the early part of the eighteenth century. When he was nine his father, Louis-Auguste, who had made his living until then by dealing in hats, bought the only bank in the city, a transaction which was to bring him a considerable fortune. Cézanne's ancestry and the character of his family and home, their place in the local community, the circle of his friendships, all these have an unusually important role not only in the formation of his personality but in the detailed moulding of his creative intentions and behaviour. His fierce and often brutal independence and his passionate impulsiveness were not only typical of the temperament of a region where his family had lived for so many generations, but may also be explained by the unpopularity of his parents in the city, occasioned by his father's financial success. The bourgeois framework of his later life, which was to sustain him through the anxieties and pressures of his artistic pilgrimage, was that natural to a prosperous middle-class family.

His studies at school — and he was a capable, hard-working pupil winning prizes for mathematics and history, as well as Greek and Latin — prepared him for the stringent disciplines he was later to impose upon himself. His chief boyhood companion was Emile Zola who, in one form or another, has left the most detailed and suggestive account we have of the youth of any great artist. We learn through him of Cézanne's excitable, enthusiastic and saturnine temperament, his way of quickly rising into anger or falling into gloom, his intense appetite for life and for the experiences both of nature and art which he shared not only with Zola but with another companion, Baptistin Baille, later to become an engineer.

The engagement of the three boys with the landscape of the region seems to have been no less devoted than Wordsworth's enjoyment of the Lakes, and in Zola's prose we hear echoes of 'The Prelude'. 'In the winter we adored the cold, the ground hardened by frost which rang gaily, and we went to eat omelettes in neighbouring villages ... in the summer all our meetings took place at the river bank, for then we were possessed by the water.' They enjoyed an equally fervent feeling for literature and above all for the most romantic and eloquent writers of their time, with Victor Hugo as the chief hero. Cézanne, particularly in the period which followed Zola's departure for Paris in 1858, himself poured forth a stream of verse in which high-sounding seriousness was mixed with fun and irony; he planned, at this time, to write a five-act drama to be called 'Henry VIII of England'.

The circumstances of his boyhood, then, provided him with an immensely valuable and deep-laid cache of experience without which he could not have sustained his subsequent career, for at this early age he became firmly anchored to art and to nature.

He came to feel a certainty of such physical presences as Mount Sainte-Victoire or his father's substantial house, the Jas de Bouffan, upon which so much of his painting was to be founded. These were to be the strong securities upon which his unquiet, exploratory spirit could depend.

It was not until he was nearly twenty that Cézanne's determination to become a painter took possession of him. By 1860 he had persuaded his father to accept this as his vocation, and whatever may have been Zola's failure of sympathy and understanding in late years, at this time he was a provider of stout and positive encouragement. In April 1861, having studied for two years in the Free Drawing Academy at Aix, Cézanne arrived for the first time in Paris where he went to work at the Atelier Suisse. The following period of six months before his return to Provence and his father's office was a time of drab discouragement, but by the end of 1862, and after a phase of further indecision, he finally committed himself to painting and to a return to Paris.

The next ten years, shared between that city and Provence, were also the formative years of Impressionism, beginning with the famous Salon des Refusés of 1863 and culminating in the First Impressionist Exhibition of 1874. In this time Cézanne came to know the leading exponents of the new art, Manet and Pissarro in particular; he was associated with them in their trials and struggles and involved in the controversies and critical debates which attended their development, but it was not until the very end of this time that he was to follow their artistic direction. The transformation of his painting to one based upon Impressionism and a central use of colour, foreshadowed by a work such as *The railway cutting* of 1869 (now in Munich), was finally accomplished when he was staying with Camille Pissarro at Pontoise in 1872—73. The first masterpiece of the new phase was to be *The house of the hanged man* (Plate vi).

He called his friend 'the humble and colossal Pissarro', and Lawrence Gowing has rightly suggested that only someone who was possessed of humility as well as profound artistic seriousness and authority could have influenced such a passionate and obstinately determined individual as Cézanne.

The period of his twenties, which was to end thus at Pontoise and Auvers, might paradoxically be described as the one in which his personality found its most direct artistic utterance. The dark, impulsive, poeticising youth, which we can see in Zola's portrait of the young Cézanne, found itself in the dark, wild, Baroque and often melodramatic pictures of this time. At this period the spirit of his personality flamed nakedly as in a lamp; thereafter its energy was relatively concealed and drove a complex mechanism of objective exploration and pictorial thought. Thereafter the force of his passion was not translated directly into images but was the source of his artistic persistence, stamina and survival. The fact that many of these early pictures, like *The black clock* (Plate iv), are so noble and possessive is not only that they are the first experiments of a great painter but because of their extreme concentration and vitality. Their fundamental darkness (for their source, as with the work of Rembrandt or Caravaggio, is shadow rather than light), their abrupt transitions of tone and their rich, corrugated pigment not only show an emergent artist's struggle to master his art but are the direct translation of his energy and introspection.

It is said that when Cézanne was working in these early years at the Atelier Suisse he found it impossible to draw direct from the living model, but had to construct the nude figure in the quiet of his studio, and this was probably a reflection not just of his anxiety in the face of a difficult natural form but of his emotional response to the presence of a living creature which had been the vehicle and focus of so much painting and poetry. There is a great similarity between the character of these early pictures and what Zola achieved in his fiction, a realism based upon observation of common life but composed and presented in terms of dramatic conventions which are something quite distinct from the plain current of events. Zola, however objective his intentions, never escaped from this kind of Romanticism, and that is perhaps the main reason why in every sense he was to lose touch with his friend.

The following thirty-five years brought Cézanne hardly any more critical or material success, for his work continued to be attacked and misunderstood by all but a few friends and perceptive sympathisers. Even his friends wrote or spoke of him, quite justly, as a man set apart, detached by the loneliness of his enquiries, so that Van Gogh, working only a few hours away from Cézanne's painting-ground, can write of him as if he belonged to another age and another continent. In an elusive way the structure of his artistic life had changed with the revelations of the 1870's. Hitherto, his way can be described as the painful ascent of a mountain ridge, the path circuitous and strewn with obstacles, but his progress supported by guides. From the moment he reached the top of that ascent he found stretched before him a flat and pathless wilderness with one conspicuous destination upon the distant horizon. The way was straighter but no less, if differently, arduous, and no companionship could assist him.

If we seek to understand the art of his maturity we must begin with that classic sentence which not only epitomises Cézanne's artistic philosophy but has been one of the founding sentences of modern taste and criticism. 'Art is a harmony, parallel with the harmony of nature.' He intended by the 'harmony of nature' not, I believe, anything as Platonic as an order of abstract forms underlying the appearance and material substance of nature. In another and equally influential dictum which begins, 'Treat nature by the cylinder, the sphere, the cone . . .' the word 'treat' is most significant, because he was surely thinking of these elemental volumes not as the explanation and source of natural objects but as a guide to the pictorial rendering of them. (He has said elsewhere that practice in the construction of these volumes should form the beginning of a painter's training.) He had, indeed, a more Goethean acceptance of the validity and truth of immediate perception, as is suggested by the words 'sensations form the foundation of my work'. But if the sensation of nature was the foundation, natural experience required to be set in order and put under rational restraint. 'All things, particularly in art, are theory developed and applied in contact with nature.' And such was not a philosophy of nature but of the parallel world of art, a theory of pictorial design and formal relationships. 'Painting is not only to copy the object, it is to seize a harmony between numerous relations.'

As Cézanne wrote of the process of humanising a landscape through the exercise of an artist's feelings, so he clearly considered the power to create pictorial harmony as something not altogether rational. 'One can do good things without being much of a harmonist or colourist. It is sufficient to have a sense of art.' And that sense embraced, no doubt, what he called taste.

The demon with which he constantly struggled was the kaleidoscopic force which nature afforded through perception and which was enhanced by his passionate temperament. 'I cannot attain the intensity that is unfolded before my senses.' That confession is a sign both of his modesty and his sincere integrity. But it was impossible for him, in spite of deliberate withdrawal from social and artistic circles and his critical attitude towards the art of his time, to isolate himself either from the contemporary current of painting which had, in the 1870's, transformed his own practice, or from the ideological climate of his age. And so he proposed that 'our art should give to nature the thrill of continuance with the appearance of all changes'. This observation explains his stated wish to make of Impressionism something as enduring as the art of the museums, the one the modern embodiment of motion, flux and the instability of physical events, the other a witness to an eternal and stable monumentality. He had to admit the impossibility for him of bringing together a group of living models to enact a Poussin-like composition in open-air circumstances which would present to his eyes the actual, vibrant conditions of nature and of natural light, with its atmospheric restlessness.

'The whole of painting' — the whole problem of painting, that is — 'is there, to yield to the atmosphere or to resist it. To yield is to deny local colours. To resist it is to give them force and variety. Titian and Veronese work by "localities" and that is what colourists do.' And so his art was to be essentially colouristic. 'Drawing and colour are not separate, everything in nature being coloured. The more the colour harmonises, the more the drawing becomes precise.' The structural coherence of solid forms, of an apple or a human head, depends upon a harmonised orchestration of colour, and without such coherence of form, drawing, which was for him the creation of volumes and not the definition of imaginary outlines, becomes slack and inexpressive. But colour is not only the means of forming volumes, but also, through its inherent tonality, the way of rendering space. 'I want to render perspective solely by means of colour.'

Such a comprehensive use of colour, which is by its nature the most dynamic, subtle and demanding of all the painter's tools, brought with it not only the struggles and anxieties which typify his career but those distinctive distortions which so troubled his contemporaries. 'The sensations of colour which give light are the reasons for the abstractions which prevent me either covering my canvas or continuing the delineation of objects when their points of contact are fine and delicate.' If his grappling with the intensity of his sensational impressions was one source of his creative agony, then an equally important one was the striving to resolve the complex equation of colour equals coloured volume plus light plus space which he had imposed upon himself. For he had set out to encompass not some general harmony but such a complex, concentrated and profoundly subtle unity that the slightest failure of observation, understanding or control could bring disaster. 'There must not be a single link too loose, not a crevice through which may escape the emotion, the light, the truth.'

This profound and terrifying ideal explains not only why, as he said, 'I advance all my canvas at one time together', but why his painting demanded the whole of his being acting together at a point of maximum concentration, why his life was so arduous why his moments of despair were large and why so many of his pictures show the marks of struggle, correction or an ultimate surrender to a necessary incompleteness, features which only the wisest in his time, most of them fellow-painters, could regard as anything but a failure of skill or understanding or as a clumsy groping towards unworthy ends.

If these were the main artistic ideas and procedures which formed his painting, how do we experience the result of them in front of the pictures? Cézanne was accustomed, in talking about painting, to make a slight but eloquent gesture, here described by his friend Emile Bernard, in this way. 'I have my motif. (He joins his hands.) A motif, you see, is this. (He draws his hands apart, fingers spread out, and brings them together again, slowly; then joins them, presses them together and contracts them, making them interlace.) There you have it; that is what one must attain.' It is not too fanciful, I believe, to compare this action and the image it creates with the structure of a Gothic cathedral. Gothic has visually been the most dynamic form of architectural expression just because its structural components declare their presence, purpose and activity so explicitly. Vault, pier, aspiring arch and flying buttress combine in an energetic contest of thrust and counter-thrust. Cézanne's art has often been called classical, but its harmony is dynamic. The *Bathers* (Plate xlvi) is not a Roman, a Raphaelesque structure, but a Gothic one, for the absent meeting of the arching tree trunks will form not a rounded but a pointed arch. The passive calm of post and lintel does not belong to Cézanne's art.

Another source of his unique expressiveness is the radiance of his pictures. From edge to edge of the canvas they emit an intense chromatic glow reminiscent of Byzantine mosaics and, in European oil painting, not so much his favourite Venetians but such a late work of Rembrandt as the Brunswick family group. The sensationalist psychology of the nineteenth century explained man's visual perceptions in terms not of objects but of spots of colour which the mind orders into the form of our mental experience, and we find an echo of this in the following statement by Cézanne: 'I take from left and right, here, there, everywhere; tones, colours, shades, I fix them, I bring them together. They make lines. They become objects, rocks, trees, without my thinking about it. They take on volume. They acquire value. If these volumes, these values, correspond on my canvas, in my feeling, to the planes and patches of colour which are there before my eyes, very good. My canvas joins hands.'

In spite of its radiance, Cézanne's painting does not provide the brash brilliance of Expressionism or Fauvism, in which every colour seems to possess the same quality of brightness, but a subtly differentiated intensity which respects the particular dynamism of each colour. The components, the bricks, from which his pictures are built are, then, the coloured touches, and in his finest paintings they operate singly as tones in a melodic line and in consort, voicing one marvellously orchestrated statement of pictorial harmony, massive and spacious. The function of his *taches* was to become quite distinct from those of Impressionism, which, having to give up their separate vitality in the cause of a general luminosity, do not play so forcefully upon our sensations. In the Cézannes of the 1870's, such as the *Portrait of Victor Chocquet* (Plate ix), the coloured touches are so physically substantial that they suggest the density of the subject, while their varying direction is used not only to enhance the modelling but to indicate the inclination of the planes. Later, and particularly after the mid-nineties, the strokes of the brush generally became less descriptive, and the pattern of their almost vertical movement makes the objects emerge in exactly the way Cézanne describes in the passage quoted above.

The one element in the objective world with which Cézanne was hardly concerned was texture and the quality of surface. His *taches* do not explain the nature of anything's skin, but they do differentiate between the special qualities of different masses, the difference in this respect between an apple and a ginger jar.

After its splendid chromatic character the most typical feature of Cézanne's art lies in his treatment of space. As might be expected in a man whose chief tool is colour, the pictures are not governed by the laws of central perspective or controlled by a single vanishing point. The eye is directed into the structure of the subject along various lines of advance, and if we associate our visual experience of the pictures with what we know of Cézanne's procedure we may appreciate his intentions. We must think of him subjecting every part of every subject to the most intense and specific scrutiny, so that every section acquires an identical significance. Each element in the picture comes to have its own spatial location and environment connected by colour with all the other elements in his design. As his paintings are constructions in terms of colour, in which every object is allowed to express itself with the same intensity, they are relatively shallow in depth, the sky where it occurs being as substantial as a rock, or the earth.

What disturbed Cézanne's contemporaries most and raised the scorn of his critical enemies were those deformities and distortions of form which seemed arbitrary and unintelligent — the lop-sided jars and bottles, those precariously slanting planes, those inequalities between one part of an object and another. Something of this is to be explained by the concept of spatial projection mentioned above, but it also arose from his acute and fastidious sense of pictorial unity which constantly demanded these modifications as the very condition of organic unity within the work.

Cézanne has declared his essential artistic intentions as clearly as any painter, and the sensations we receive in front of his work are powerful and explicit. What remains, and probably always will remain, elusive is the exact nature of his methods, which are the cause of constant debate and disagreement. But we, fifty-five years after his death, are better placed to understand how comprehensive an artist he was, than those who immediately followed him and who, as artists or critics, used his art to defend their own concepts. He is not to be explained or appreciated in terms simply of significant form, but only by recognising the presence of those three elements which he struggled so hard to unite, nature, art and that inner personal life of sensation and feeling which knew the whole gamut of experience, from joy to despair.

1

11

IV

V

VI

VII

VIII

Outline Biography of Cézanne

1839   January 19th. Born in Aix-en-Provence.

1849–52   Ecole St Joseph in Aix.

1852–58   Attends College Bourbon in Aix. Begins a friendship with Emile Zola.

1858–59   Working in the Drawing Academy in Aix.

1859   Studies Law in the University at Aix. His father acquires the Jas de Bouffan, the subject of numerous paintings by Cézanne.

1861   Abandons Law studies and goes to Paris to paint, but returns in the same year, discouraged.

1862   Returns again to Paris and fails to gain admittance to the Ecole des Beaux-Arts.

1863   Exhibits in the Salon des Refusés.
Between 1863 and 1870 works in Aix, Paris and L'Estaque (where he lived with Hortense Fiquet, a model and mother of his son).

1872   Moves to Pontoise, where he lives near Pissarro, is influenced by him, and begins to paint according to Impressionism.

1873   Moves to Auvers-sur-Oise. Here he becomes friendly with Dr Gachet. (Gachet was a supporter of the moderns and looked after Van Gogh in his last years.)

1874   Participates in the First Impressionist Exhibition.
From 1874 to 1899 he works either in Paris or in Aix with occasional visits elsewhere.

1886	His father dies, leaving him a sizeable fortune, including Jas de Bouffan.
1892	Emile Bernard publishes a pamphlet on his work.
1895	Cézanne has his first one-man show organised by Vollard at the instigation of Pissarro.
1899	Much to the distress of Cézanne the Jas de Bouffan has to be sold to settle his father's estate. He rents an apartment in Aix. From 1900 he works almost exclusively in Aix until his death on 22nd October, 1906.
1902	Has a new studio built on a hill dominating Aix and moves in the following year.
1906	Dies following a fainting attack during a storm in which he was working out of doors. He was brought back on a laundry cart, and congestion of the liver resulted from the chill he caught. He is buried in Aix-en-Provence cemetery.

Cézanne on Himself and his Art

A selection from his letters

I am beginning to consider myself stronger than all those around me, and you know that the good opinion I have of myself has only been reached after mature consideration. I have still got to work, not so as to be able to add the final polish, that is for the admiration of imbeciles. And the thing that is commonly so much appreciated is merely the reality of the handwork and renders all work resulting from it inartistic and common. I must strive after perfection only for the pleasure of giving added truth and learning. And believe me, the hour always comes when one makes an impression and one has admirers far more fervent and convinced than those who are only flattered by the empty appearances.

To the artist's mother.
26th September, 1874.

Monsieur Chocquet who spoke to me about them . . . It is like a playing card – red roofs over the blue sea. If the weather is favourable I may perhaps carry them through to the end. Up to the present I have done nothing. – But motifs could be found which would require three or four months' work, for the vegetation does not change here. The olive and pine trees are the ones which always preserve their foliage. The sun is so terrific here that it seems to me as if the objects were silhouetted not only in black and white, but in blue, red, brown and violet. I may be mistaken, but this seems to me to be the opposite of modelling.

To Camille Pissarro.
2nd July, 1876.

I should have wished to possess the intellectual equilibrium that characterises you and permits you to achieve without fail the desired end . . . Chance has not favoured me with an equal self-assurance, it is the only regret I have about things of this earth. With regard to the rest I have nothing to complain of. Always it is the sky, the things without limits that attract me and give me the opportunity of looking at them with pleasure.

But as regards the realisation of the most simple wishes, which seem as if they should proceed by themselves, a luckless fate is apparently present to impair success;

I had a few vineyards but unseasonable frost came and cut the thread of my hopes. Whereas my wish on the contrary was for them to flower, and so I can only wish that your plantations shall flourish and your vegetation develop well: green being one of the gayest colours which is the most soothing to the eyes. To conclude I must tell you that I still go on with my painting and that this country here, which has never found an interpreter worthy of the richness it harbours, contains many treasures to be gathered.

To Victor Chocquet.
11th May, 1886.

... the many studies I made having given only negative results, I had resolved to work in silence until the day when I should feel myself able to defend in theory the results of my attempts.

To Octave Maus.
27th November, 1889.

If I am not mistaken you appeared to be very angry with me. Could you but see inside me, the man within, you would be so no longer. Do you not see to what a sad state I am reduced. Not master of myself, a man who does not exist, and it is you, who claim to be a philosopher, who would cause my final downfall? But I curse the X ... s and the few rascals who, for the sake of writing an article for fifty francs, drew the attention of the public to me. All my life I have worked to be able to earn my living, but I thought that one could do good painting without attracting attention to one's private life. To be sure an artist wishes to raise his standard intellectually as much as possible, but the man must remain in obscurity. Pleasure must be found in the studying. If it had been given to me to succeed, I should have remained in my corner with my few studio companions with whom we used to go out for a pint ... You are young, and I can understand that you wish to succeed. But for me, what is there left for me to do in my position but submit? And were it not that I am passionately fond of the contours of this country, I should not be here.

To Joachim Gasquet.
30th April, 1896.

Monsieur,

The rather discourteous manner with which you take the liberty of entering my room is not calculated to please me. In the future please see that you are announced.

Please give the glass and the canvas which were left in your studio to the person who comes for them.

To Louis Le Bail.
1898.

X

XII

XIII

XIV

XV

XVI

It seems to me that I find it difficult to dissociate myself from the young people who have shown themselves to be so much in sympathy with me, and I do not think that I shall in any way harm the course of my studies by exhibiting.

To Ambroise Vollard.
17th March, 1902.

I have made some progress. Why so late and with such difficulty? Is art really a priest-hood that demands the pure in heart who must belong to it entirely?

To Ambroise Vollard.
9th January, 1903.

In your letter you speak of my realisation in art. I think that every day I am attaining it more, although with some difficulty. For if the strong experience of nature – and assuredly I have it – is the necessary basis for all conception of art on which rests the grandeur and beauty of all future work, the knowledge of the means of expressing our emotion is no less essential, and is only to be acquired through very long experience.

The approbation of others is a stimulus of which, however, one must sometimes be wary. The feeling of one's own strength renders one modest.

To Louis Aurenche.
25th January, 1904.

May I repeat what I told you here: treat nature by the cylinder, the sphere, the cone, everything in proper perspective so that each side of an object or a plane is directed towards a central point. Lines parallel to the horizon give breadth, that is a section of nature, or if you prefer, of the spectacle that the *Pater Omnipotens Æterne Deus* spreads out before our eyes. Lines perpendicular to this horizon give depth. But nature for us men is more depth than surface, whence the need of introducing into our light vibrations, represented by reds and yellows, a sufficient amount of blue to give the impression of air.

To Emile Bernard.
15th April, 1904.

I am progressing very slowly, for nature reveals herself to me in very complex forms; and the progress needed is incessant. One must see one's model correctly and experience it in the right way; and furthermore express oneself forcibly and with distinction.

Taste is the best judge. It is rare. Art only addresses itself to an excessively small number of individuals.

The artist must scorn all judgement that is not based on an intelligent observation of character. He must beware of the literary spirit which so often causes painting to deviate from its true path – the concrete study of nature – to lose itself all too long in intangible speculations.

The Louvre is a good book to consult, but it must only be an intermediary. The real and immense study that must be taken up is the manifold picture of nature.

To Emile Bernard.
12th May, 1904.

Painters must devote themselves entirely to the study of nature and try to produce pictures which are an instruction. Talks on art are almost useless. The work which goes to bring progress in one's own subject is sufficient compensation for the incomprehension of imbeciles.

Literature expresses itself by abstractions, whereas painting, by means of drawing and colour, gives concrete shape to sensations and perceptions. One is neither too scrupulous nor too sincere nor too submissive to nature; but one is more or less master of one's model, and, above all, of the means of expression. Get to the heart of what is before you and continue to express yourself as logically as possible.

To Emile Bernard.
26th May, 1904.

To achieve progress nature alone counts, and the eye is trained through contact with her. It becomes concentric by looking and working. I mean to say that in an orange, an apple, a bowl, a head, there is a culminating point; and this point is always – in spite of the tremendous effect of light and shade and colourful sensations – the closest to our eye; the edges of the objects recede to a centre on our horizon. With a small temperament one can be very much of a painter. One can do good things without being very much of a harmonist or a colourist. It is sufficient to have a sense of art – and this sense is doubtless the horror of the bourgeois. Therefore, institutions, pensions, honours, can only be made for cretins, rogues and rascals. Do not be an art critic, but paint, therein lies salvation.

To Emile Bernard.
25th July, 1904.

Studying the model and realising it is sometimes very slow in coming for the artist.

Whoever the master is whom you prefer, this must only be a directive for you. Otherwise you will never be anything but an imitator. With any feeling for nature whatever, and some fortunate gifts – and you have some – you should be able to dissociate yourself; advice, the methods of another, must not make you change your own manner of feeling. Should you at the moment be under the influence of one who is older than you, believe me, as soon as you begin to feel yourself, your own emotions will finally emerge and conquer their place in the sun – *get the upper hand*, confidence – what you must strive to attain is a good method of *construction* . . .

Michelangelo is a constructor, and Rafael an *artist* who, great as he is, is always limited by the model. When he tries to be thoughtful he falls below the *niveau* of his great rival.
To Charles Camoin.
9th December, 1904.

Yes, I approve of your admiration for the strongest of all the Venetians; we are celebrating Tintoretto. Your desire to find a moral, an intellectual point of support in the works, which assuredly we shall never surpass, makes you continually on the *qui vive*, searching incessantly for the way that you dimly apprehend, which will lead you surely to the recognition in front of nature, of what your means of expression are; and the day you will have found them, be convinced that you will find also, without effort and in front of nature, the means employed by the four or five great ones of Venice.

This is true without possible doubt – I am very positive: – an optical impression is produced on our organs of sight which makes us classify as light, half-tone or quarter-tone, the surfaces represented by colour sensations. (So that light does not exist for the painter.) As long as we are forced to proceed from black to white, the first of these abstractions being like a point of support for the eye as much as for the mind, we are confused, we do not succeed in mastering ourselves, in possessing ourselves.
To Emile Bernard.
23rd December, 1904.

My age and my health will never allow me to realise the dream of art that I have been pursuing all my life. But I shall always be grateful to the public of intelligent amateurs who had – despite my own hesitations – the intuition of what I wanted to attempt for the renewal of my art. To my mind one should not substitute oneself for the past, one has merely to add a new link. With the temperament of a painter and an ideal of art, that is to say, a conception of nature, sufficient powers of expression would have been necessary to be intelligible for man and to occupy a suitable position in the history of art.
To Roger Marx.
23rd January, 1905.

As you write, I think I really have made some slight progress in the last studies that you saw at my house. It is, however, very painful to have to register that the improvement produced in the comprehension of nature from the point of view of the form of the picture and the development of the means of expression should be accompanied by old age and a weakening of the body.

The Louvre is the book in which we learn to read. We must not, however, be satisfied with retaining the beautiful formulas of our illustrious predecessors. Let us go forth to study beautiful nature, let us try to free our minds from them, let us strive to express ourselves according to our personal temperaments. Time and reflection, moreover, modify, little by little, our vision, and at last comprehension comes to us.

To Emile Bernard.
1905.

Now, being old, nearly 70 years, the sensations of colour, which give light, are the reason for the abstractions which prevent me from either covering my canvas or continuing the delimitation of the objects when their points of contact are fine and delicate; from which it results that my image or picture is incomplete. On the other hand, the planes are placed one on top of the other from whence neo-impressionism emerged, which outlines the contours with a black stroke, a failing that must be fought at all costs. Well, nature, when consulted, gives us the means of attaining this end.

To Emile Bernard.
23rd October, 1905.

Finally I must tell you that as a painter I am becoming more clear-sighted in front of nature, but that with me the realisation is always very difficult. I cannot attain the intensity that is unfolded before my senses. I have not the magnificent richness of colouring that animates nature. Here on the edge of the river, the motifs are very plentiful, the same subject seen from a different angle gives a subject for study of the highest interest and so varied that I think I could be occupied for months without changing my place, simply bending a little more to the right or left.

To his son.
8th September, 1906.

From *Paul Cézanne Letters*, edited by John Rewald, translated from the French by Marguerite Kay, Cassirer, Oxford, 1946

XVII

XVIII

XIX

XX

XXII

XXIII

Cézanne as seen by his Contemporaries

Monsieur Cézanne is from Provence and is like the man from the Midi whom Daudet describes: 'When first I saw him I thought he looked like a cut-throat with large red eyeballs standing out from his head in a most ferocious manner, a rather fierce-looking pointed beard, quite grey, and an excited way of talking that positively made the dishes rattle.' I found later on that I had misjudged his appearance, for far from being fierce or cut-throat, he has the gentlest manner possible, 'comme un enfant', as he would say. His manners at first rather startled me – he scrapes his soup plate, then lifts it and pours the remaining drops in his spoon; he even takes his chop in his fingers and pulls the meat from the bone. He eats with his knife and accompanies every gesture, every movement of his hand, with that implement, which he grasps firmly when he commences his meal and never puts down until he leaves the table. Yet in spite of the total disregard of the dictionary of manners, he shows a politeness towards us which no other man here would have shown. He will not allow Louise to serve him before us in the usual order of succession at the table; he is even deferential to that stupid maid, and he pulls off the old tam-o-shanter, which he wears to protect his bald head, when he enters the room . . .

   Cézanne is one of the most liberal artists I have ever seen. He prefaces every remark with: 'Pour moi' it is so and so, but he grants that everyone may be as honest and as true to nature from their convictions; he doesn't believe that everyone should see alike.   Mary Cassatt (from a letter dated 1894)

At Vollard's there is a very complete exhibition of Cézanne's works. Still lifes of astonishing perfection, and some unfinished works really extraordinary for their fierceness and character. I don't imagine they will be understood . . .

I also thought of Cézanne's show in which there were exquisite things, still lifes of irreproachable perfection, others *much worked on* and yet unfinished, of even greater beauty, landscapes, nudes and heads that are unfinished but yet grandiose, and so *painted*, so supple . . . Why? Sensation is there! . . .

   Curiously enough, while I was admiring this strange disconcerting aspect of Cézanne, familiar to me for many years, Renoir arrived. But my enthusiasm was nothing compared with Renoir's. Degas himself is seduced by the charm of this refined savage, Monet, all of us . . . Are we mistaken? I don't think so. The only ones who are not subject to the charm of Cézanne are precisely those artists or collectors who have shown by their errors that their sensibilities are defective. They properly point out the faults we all see, which leap to the eye, but the charm – that they do not see. As Renoir said so well, these paintings have I do not know what quality; like the things of Pompeii, so crude and so admirable! . . .

Camille Pissarro: *Letters to Lucien*

Ripe grapes overflow the edges of a shallow dish; on the cloth bright green and violet-red apples are mingled. The whites are blue and the blues are white. A devil of a painter, this Cézanne!

Cézanne paints a brilliant landscape: ultramarine background, heavy greens, glistening ochres: a row of trees, their branches interlaced, allowing, however, a glimpse of the house of his friend Zola, with its vermilion shutters turned orange by the yellow reflected from the walls. The burst of emerald greens expresses the delicate verdure of the garden, while in contrast the deep note of the purple nettles in the foreground orchestrates the simple poem. It is at Médan.

A pretentious passer-by takes an astonished glance at what he thinks is some amateur's pitiful mess and, smiling like a professor, says to Cézanne: 'You paint?'

'Certainly, but not very much.'

'Oh, I can see that. Look here, I'm an old pupil of Corot's; and if you'll allow me, I can put that in its proper place for you with a few skilful touches. Values, values . . . that's the whole thing!'

And the vandal impudently spreads his imbecilites over the brilliant canvas. Dirty greys cover the Oriental silks.

'How happy you must be, Monsieur!' cries Cézanne. 'When you do a portrait I have no doubt you put the shine on the end of the nose as you do on the legs of the chair.'

Cézanne seizes his palette, and with his knife scrapes off all Monsieur's dirty mud. Then, after a moment of silence, he lets a tremendous . . . and turning to Monsieur, says, 'Oh! what a relief.'

Paul Gauguin: *Intimate Journals*, translated by Van Wyck Brooks, Heinemann, London, 1930

50

Instinctively these days I keep remembering what I have seen of Cézanne's, because he has rendered so forcibly – as in the 'Harvest' we saw at Portier's – the harsh side of Provence. It has become very different from what it was in spring . . . I'm thinking of what Portier used to say, that seen by themselves, the Cézannes he had didn't look like anything else, but put near other pictures, they washed the colour out of everything else. He also used to say that the Cézannes did well in gold, which means that the colour scheme was pitched very high . . .

The country near Aix, where Cézanne works, is just the same as this, it is still the Crau. If coming home with my canvas, I say to myself, 'Look! I've got the very tones of old Cézanne!' I only mean that Cézanne, like Zola, is so absolutely part of the countryside and knows it so intimately, that you must make the same calculations in your head to arrive at the same tones. Of course, if you saw them side by side, mine would hold their own, but there would be no resemblance . . .

I think that the continual wind here must have something to do with the haggard look the painted studies have. Because you see it in Cézanne too . . .

If you saw my canvases, what would you say of them? You won't find the almost timid, conscientious brush stroke of Cézanne in them. But as I am now painting the same landscape, Crau and Camargue – though at a slightly different spot – there may well remain certain connections in it in the matter of colour. I couldn't help thinking of Cézanne from time to time, at exactly those moments when I realised how clumsy his touch in certain studies is – excuse the word clumsy – seeing that he probably did these studies when the mistral was blowing. As half the time I am faced with the same difficulties, I get an idea of why Cézanne's touch is sometimes so sure, whereas at other times it appears awkward. It's his easel that's reeling . . .

Cézanne is a respectable married man, just like the old Dutchmen; if there is plenty of male potency in his work, it is because he does not let it evaporate in merry-making.

Vincent van Gogh: *Letters to Theo*

Later Comments on Cézanne

It would be untrue to say that he had no talent, but whereas the intention of Manet and of Monet and of Degas was always to paint, the intention of Cézanne was, I am afraid, never very clear to himself. His work may be described as the anarchy of painting, as art in delirium. It is impossible to deny to this strange being a certain uncouth individuality, otherwise no one would remember them. I pause to ask myself which I would prefer, one of Millet's conventional, simpering peasants or one of Cézanne's crazy cornfields, peopled with violent reapers, reapers from bedlam. I think that I prefer Cézanne.

George Moore: *Reminiscences of the Impressionist Painters*, Maunsel, Dublin, 1906

One has the impression that each of these objects is infallibly in its place, and that its place was ordained for it from the beginning of all things, so majestically and serenely does it repose there. Such phrases are, of course, rather fantastic, but one has to make use of figurative expressions to render at all the extraordinary feeling of gravity and solemnity which the artist has found how to evoke from the presentment of these commonplace objects. One suspects a strange complicity between these objects, as though they insinuated mysterious meanings by the way they are extended on the plane of the table and occupy the imagined picture space. Each form seems to have a surprising amplitude, to permit of our apprehending it with an ease which surprises us, and yet they admit a free circulation in the surrounding space. It is above all the main directions given by the rectilinear lines of the napkin and the knife that make us feel so vividly this horizontal extension. And this horizontal supports the spherical volumes, which enforce, far more than real apples could, the sense of their density and mass . . .

We may describe the process by which such a picture is arrived at in some such way as this: the actual objects presented to the artist's vision are first deprived of all those specific characters by which we ordinarily apprehend their concrete existence – they are reduced to pure elements of space and volume. In this abstract world these elements are perfectly co-ordinated and organized by the artist's sensual intelligence, they attain logical consistency. These abstractions are then brought back into the concrete world

XXV

XXVI

XXVII

XXIX

XXXII

of real things, not by giving them back their specific peculiarities but by expressing them in an incessantly varying and shifting texture. They retain their abstract intelligibility, their amenity to the human mind, and regain that reality of actual things which is absent from all abstractions.

Of course in laying all this out one is falsifying the actual processes of the artist's mind. In reality, the processes go on simultaneously and unconsciously – indeed the unconsciousness is essential to the nervous vitality of the texture. No doubt all great art arrives at some such solution of the apparently insoluble problems of artistic creation. Here in certain works of Cézanne we seem to get a particularly clear vision of the process of such creations . . .

Of all Cézanne's portraits perhaps that of M. Geffroy is the most celebrated . . . The equilibrium so consummately achieved results from the counterpoise of a great number of directions. One has only to imagine what would happen if the books on the shelf behind the sitter's head were upright, like the others, to realize upon what delicate adjustments the solidity of this amazing structure depends. One cannot think of many designs where so complex a balance is so securely held. The mind of the spectator is held in a kind of thrilled suspense by the unsuspected correspondences of all these related elements. One is filled with wonder at an imagination capable of holding in so firm a grasp all these disparate objects, this criss-cross of plastic movements and directions. Perhaps, however, in order to avoid exaggeration, one ought to admit that since Cézanne's day other constructions have been made as complex and as well poised, but this has I think been accomplished at too great a sacrifice of the dictates of sensibility, with too great a denial of vital quality in the forms.

Roger Fry: *Cézanne*, Hogarth Press Ltd., London, 1930

Cézanne was not a great classic: he was an artist, often clumsy, always in difficulties, very limited in his range, absurdly so in his most numerous productions, but with 'quite a little mood', and the haunting idea of an art built upon the early Manet, at which he could only hint. He oscillated between Manet's earlier and finer manner, that of marked contours and broadly decided colour, and a painting based on the early Monet, all colour in a high key. In this manner he produced certain landscapes, tender and beautiful in colour, but the figure was too difficult for him, and from difficulties of all sorts he escaped into the still lifes I have spoken of, flattened jugs, apples, and napkins like blue tin that would clank if they fell. What is fatal to the claim set up for him as a deliberate designer, creating eternal images out of the momentary lights of the

Impressionists, is the fact that his technique remains that of the Impressionists, a sketcher's technique, adapted for snatching hurriedly at effects that will not wait. Hence his touch, hence those slops of form out of which he tries to throw a figure together. No one was ever further from logical 'classic' construction, if that is what we are looking for; none of the Impressionists was so uncertain in his shots at a shape. And when we come to fundamentals, to rhythm, whether it be the rhythm of the thing seen, or the rhythm of the picture imagined . . . Cézanne is helpless.

D. S. Macoll: *Confessions of a Keeper*, Maclehose, London, 1931

Cézanne was fated, as his passion was immense, to be immensely neglected, immensely misunderstood, and now, I think, immensely overrated . . . after all acknowledgement has been made of a certain greatness in his talent. The moral weight of his single-hearted and unceasing effort, of his sublime love for his art, has made itself felt. In some mysterious way, indeed, this gigantic sincerity impresses and holds even those who have not the slightest knowledge of what were his qualities, of what he was driving at, what he achieved, or of where he failed . . . The difficulties that a painter must always experience with the Cézanne cult are the very real beauty of the tiny percentage of Cézanne's successes, and the immense respect and sympathy inspired by Cézanne's character and industry. To criticise him is, morally, almost like criticising an artist without arms who has aroused the very proper sympathy and patronage of royalty.

W. R. Sickert: *A Free House*, Macmillan, London, 1947

Everyone in the course of that (the 19th) century had supposed that painting was a visual art; that the painter was primarily a person who used his eyes, and used his hands only to record what the use of his eyes had revealed to him. Then came Cézanne, and began to paint like a blind man. His still-life studies, which enshrine the essence of his genius, are like groups of things that have been groped over with the hands; he uses colour not to reproduce what he sees in looking at them but to express almost in a kind of algebraic notation what in this groping he has felt . . . It is the same when Cézanne takes us into the open air. His landscapes have lost almost every trace of visuality . . . it is a perplexing mixture of projections and recessions, over and round which we find ourselves feeling our way as one can imagine an infant feeling its way, when it has barely begun to crawl, among the nursery furniture. And over the landscape broods the obsession of Mount Sainte-Victoire never looked at, but always felt, as a child feels the table over the back of its head.

R. G. Collingwood: *Principles of Art*, Oxford University Press, 1938

Cézanne's classic and symbolic triumph has nothing of the direct expressionist consummation toward which the original impetus points. We learn more about the positive force of his abstracted recreation if we look again at the opposite state, shown to us in the painting and poetry of his youth. At the crux of *Une Terrible Histoire* a woman, the most beautiful he has ever seen, calls the poet to her. Throwing himself before her, he kisses with guilty lips her breast, but on the instant the chill of death seizes him: the woman in his arms is changed to a corpse, to a rattling skeleton. The terror is real. The fantasy, though we rarely meet it so undisguised, is one that we recognize. Analysis of the pictures of Cézanne's twenties would reveal much of the same theme: their force carries a burden of grief. There was a fatality inherent in the direct embrace. The mature style made it good; it enfolded the visible world in an embrace which was itself a reparation, a lasting recreation of the object of love. In his art, as in his utterances, what is stable and durable has a special meaning. Whatever might prove transitory in his grasp was excluded from it, for the nature of change was predetermined and terrible: he could possess only a form as lasting as the art of the museums. The virtue of the living world before his eyes was that it remained real and alive. He assured himself of its continued existence at each look; each touch, owing nothing to the last, could record that its virtue was undiminished.

Lawrence Gowing (from the catalogue of the Arts Council's Cézanne Exhibition, 1954)

To us it seems that for Cézanne that moment when his eyes were crossing and recrossing the visible surfaces of the natural world, apples and ginger-jars, or trees, rocks and houses – that that was the moment when the vitally significant rhythms of his inner vision came most clearly to consciousness, suddenly projecting themselves, mirage-like, *between* the painter and the scene that he contemplated: a dancing imagery *that was the transformation* he so desperately, so persistently sought for those apples and those trees. The tension between 'inner' and 'outer' was thus perfect; the inner appearing only when he had given himself up completely to the 'study' of the outer. There is not the slightest doubt that Cézanne was in a frenzy to 'express himself', as we say. But this explosive force within was never allowed to emerge neat and undiluted. It was never allowed to flood out on to canvas as a furiously incoherent slashing and stabbing of pigment. Cézanne opposed this interior surge by a desperate discipline – he forced it to express itself entirely in terms of images of the sunlit, exterior world – images which, in their turn, also presented themselves to him with an almost overwhelming force. Therefore, his art was an equation of two great streams of experience – one from inside himself; the other from outside.

Cézanne's watercolours have given new status to their medium . . . something at once monumental and utterly delicate; aerially immense and supremely indicative of volume and sculptured form, yet intimate, sweet and clear, as all that does no violence to a paper host must be. Cézanne's watercolours are, in short, no substitute: sketch or impression would be words of little accuracy . . .

If white paper would seem to confound these remarks, I must point out how used are the white areas which lie scattered thick as archipelagoes across these pictures. I would almost say that in them the expression is at its most intense; that it is precisely the white patches that are most potent in form, almost building from the surface with the movement and light which is concentrated in them. The flakes of colour which alight in definition *round* the forms contemplated, overlap one another with rainbow richness, stating and re-stating contours and planes in the unending attempt to capture the essential aspect, the heart of form. White is where he dared not tread: the vital node of every form, where false statement would destroy the whole. White is the unstateable core of each coloured snowstorm of definitions; and its potency derives from the fact that every slanting stroke at the perimeter throws definition inwards, adds meaning to the white! . . . doubt and certainty lie side by side in every gesture of the brush; for Cézanne's humility before sensation and his overwhelming conviction in the experience of that sensation are both present, and obvious, in every picture he ever painted. Hesitation – conviction: hesitation – statement: he maintained and endured the tension like a saint, never yielding to the temptation to produce synthetic unity, to work the picture together on a level other than that of his peculiar conviction . . .

I have long known Cézanne's austerity; what attacked me lately was the great tenderness of feeling: the brilliant early foliage of the curving lane: the purple-gold light of afternoon on the mountain: the green winking of a bottle amongst the minor suns of yellow-red apples: the blue and white dazzle of morning light in the trees. So much for the theorists' abolition of 'the subject'! . . . the *significant form* of an apple derives at least as great a part of its significance from its connection with that apple as from the fact that it exists in the category of 'form'.

Patrick Heron: *The Changing Forms of Art*,
Routledge & Kegan Paul, London, 1955

XXXIV

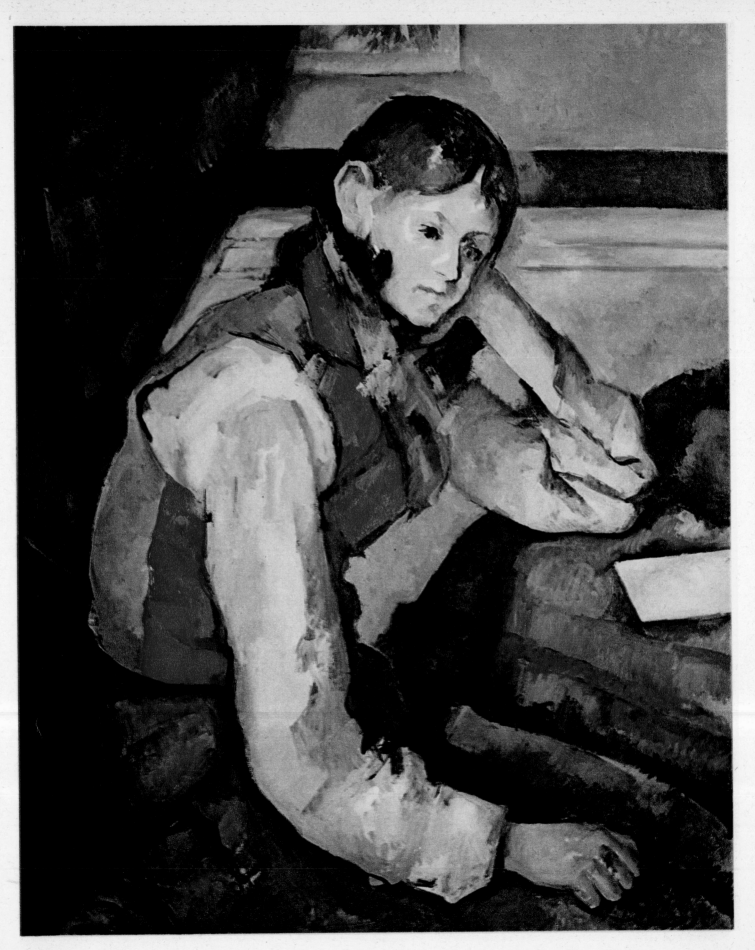

XXXVIII

Notes on the Plates
by Trewin Copplestone
(All the paintings here reproduced, unless otherwise stated, are oils on canvas.)

Plate i *Head of an old man*, 1865–8. Paris, Louvre. 20×18³/₄ in. (51×48 cm.). This very early work of Cézanne's is painted in the thick impasto of his first style. At one time it was owned by the art-dealer Ambroise Vollard.

Plate ii *Still life, skull and candlestick*, 1865–7. Switzerland, Private Collection. 18³/₄×24³/₈ in. (47.5×62.5 cm.). Another early work in thick impasto, particularly noticeable on the skull and book pages.

Plate iii *Rue des Saules, Montmartre*, 1867–9. Paris, Renand Collection. 12½×16 in. (31.5 ×40.5 cm.). A Utrillo-like subject, this is one of the paintings in what Cézanne called his 'couillarde' manner. It is not as successful as some of his portraits at this time – perhaps it did not demand of him that passionate urge of artistic expression which his use of the coarse term implies.

Plate iv *The black clock*, 1869–70. Mr & Mrs Niarchos Collection. 21¼×28³/₄ in. (54×73 cm.). This painting belonged originally to Emile Zola. It later entered the Edward G. Robinson Collection, and it is now in the collection belonging to Mr & Mrs Niarchos.

Plate v *Modern Olympia*, 1872–3. Paris, Louvre, 18×21⁵/₈ in. (46×55 cm.). Shown at the First Impressionist Exhibiton, 1874. It belonged at one time to Dr Gachet, and is one of Cézanne's important early works. He had painted another version of the same subject in 1870. On April 25th there appeared in *Charivari* an article by Louis Leroy in the form of a conversation between himself and the academic painter Joseph Vincent, 'recipient of medals and decorations under several governments'. In the article Leroy says of this painting: 'Alas, go and look at it! A woman folded in two, from whom a Negro girl is removing the last veil in order to offer her in all her ugliness to the charmed gaze of a brown puppet . . .' The 'brown puppet' is said to be Cézanne himself. Another reviewer commented: 'On Sunday the public saw fit to sneer at a fantastic figure which is revealed under an opium sky to a drug addict. This apparition of a little pink and nude flesh which is being pushed, in the empyrean cloud, by a kind of demon or incubus, like a voluptuous vision, this corner of artificial paradise, has suffocated the most courageous, and M. Cézanne merely gives the impression of being a sort of madman who paints in *delirium tremens*.'

Plate vi   *The house of the hanged man*, 1873. Paris, Louvre. 21⅞×26¼ in. (55.5×66.5 cm.). This painting is important in Cézanne's development as it is one of the first in which his desire for order becomes apparent. At this time Cézanne was living near Camille Pissarro in the village of Pontoise, and later moved to Auvers-sur-Oise. It was at Pontoise that Cézanne's Impressionist period began. During this time Pissarro and Cézanne painted much together. Cézanne had developed his slow, patient method of painting, and it is said that one day, when they were painting near one another, an old peasant told Pissarro, 'Well, sir, you have an assistant over there who isn't doing a stroke of work.' The painting was shown in the Impressionist Exhibition of 1874.

Plate vii   *View of Auvers*, 1873–5. Chicago, The Art Institute. 25½×31¾ in. (65×81 cm.). In the more rural atmosphere Cézanne could work in the open undisturbed by curious spectators whom he detested. His connection at this time with Pissarro led to a lightening of his palette, and this is almost an Impressionist painting. It does however give an indication of the monumentality of design and interpretation of form which later emerge. Cézanne had difficulty in deciding that he had finished a painting, and often his friend Dr Gachet, making the decision for him, would tell Cézanne to stop – which Cézanne, grumbling, would do.

Plate viii   *Dahlias in a Delft vase*, 1873–5. Paris, Louvre. 28¾×21¼ in. (73×54 cm.). This was painted in Dr Gachet's house, and the vase is still in the possession of the family. There is a painting by Pissarro of the same subject.

Plate ix   *Portrait of Victor Chocquet*, 1876–7. Cambridge, Lord Rothschild Collection. 18×14 in. (45.5×35.5 cm.). Chocquet was a friend and supporter of Cézanne. He was a chief customs supervisor, and his collection of paintings, when sold on his death in 1899, included thirty-five Cézannes. His portrait was also painted by Renoir. Cézanne's portrait, when exhibited in the Third Impressionist Exhibition, 1877, was described as the 'chocolate Billoir' (Billoir was a celebrated murderer of the period). Chocquet's purchases were made purely on his own tastes, regardless of investment or popularity – a true collector. Duret said of him: 'I remember having seen him try to persuade well-known critics and hostile artists who had come simply to run the show down.

This gave Chocquet a reputation, and whenever he appeared people liked to attack him on his favourite subject. He was always ready. He always had the right word when it was a question of his painter friends. He was particularly indefatigable on the subject of Cézanne whom he placed on the very highest level . . . Many were amused at Chocquet's enthusiasm which they considered something like a gentle insanity . . .

Plate x   *Still life with apples and biscuits*, c. 1877. Paris, Private Collection. $14^7/_8 \times 21\frac{1}{2}$ in. (38×55 cm.). This painting is one of a series done at this time in which a plate of biscuits and fruits figured. It is another example of Cézanne's habitual use of the same 'motifs' rearranged in different paintings.

Plate xi   *Self-portrait*, c. 1879. London, Tate Gallery. $13^3/_4 \times 10^5/_8$ in. (35×27 cm.). This work was probably painted during one of Cézanne's visits to Paris in 1879. The pattern on the wallpaper is to be seen in other paintings of this period, and was apparently in his apartment in the Rue de l'Ouest.

Plate xii   *Auvers, from the Harmé valley*, 1879–82. Zurich, Private Collection. $28^3/_4 \times 36$ in. (73×92 cm.). Cézanne stayed near Dr Gachet at Auvers at the time this picture was painted, and he did a number of studies in and around Auvers.

Plate xiii   *L'Estaque: the village and the sea*, 1878–83. Switzerland, Private Collection. $20\frac{1}{2} \times 24^3/_4$ in. (52×63 cm.). L'Estaque is on the south coast of France, near Marseilles, and is a favourite subject with Cézanne (see Plates xvii–xix). He first went to L'Estaque in 1870 – mainly, it is imagined, to avoid being drafted into the army – and after that date frequently visited it from nearby Aix, where he lived. This painting was done during a period of difficulty with his father, when he was helped financially by Zola. He worked at L'Estaque with other painters, including Renoir and Monticelli. Zola described the scenery round L'Estaque in one of his novels: 'The country is superb. The arms of rock stretch out on either side of the gulf, while the islands, extending in width, seem to bar the horizon, and the sea is but a vast basin, a lake of brilliant blue when the weather is fine . . . When the sun falls perpendicularly to the horizon, the sea, almost black, seems to sleep between the two promontories of rocks whose whiteness is relieved by yellow and brown. The pines dot the red earth with green. It is a vast panorama, a corner of the Orient rising up in the blinding vibration of the day.'

Plate xiv	*The lady with the fan* (Mme Cézanne), 1879–82. Zurich, Bührle Collection. 36¼ × 28¾ in. (92 × 73 cm.). Cézanne was very demanding of his models, and his wife, a normally talkative woman, was obliged, on pain of his displeasure, to sit silently and without moving for hours on end. She was almost his only woman sitter – perhaps not surprisingly.
Plate xv	*Poplars*, 1879–82. Paris, Louvre. 24⅜ × 30¾ in. (61.5 × 78 cm.). This is a very rich example of Cézanne's middle period when he was beginning to acquire his personal style. The short similarly directed brush strokes and the use of heavy green and brown ochre are typical of this period.
Plate xvi	*Self-portrait*, 1880–1. Paris, Louvre. 10¼ × 5⅞ in. (26 × 15 cm.). Cézanne's self-portraits are among the most revealing of his works. He painted a large number of them as well as numerous drawings, and they provide an opportunity, paralleled perhaps only in the work of Rembrandt, for examining the development of his style and his own understanding of his appearance. His baldness must, in some respects, have been a great asset, enabling him to express the volume and mass of the head unhampered by a covering of hair.
Plate xvii	*Rocks at L'Estaque*, 1882–5. Sao Paulo, Museum of Art. 28¾ × 35¾ in. (73 × 91 cm.). The bulked shape of rocks is one of Cézanne's favourite motifs. He found in the related geological structures an opportunity to emphasise the aspect of unity in his subject.
Plate xviii	*Mount Marseilleveyre*, 1882–5. Switzerland, Private Collection. 20 × 24 in. (51 × 62 cm.). Another view from L'Estaque (see Plate xiii) painted at about the same time.
Plate xix	*L'Estaque*, 1882–5. Paris, Louvre. 22¾ × 28¼ in. (58 × 72 cm.). This is a view across the Bay of Marseilles from L'Estaque.
Plate xx	*The little bridge, Mennency*, 1882–5. Paris, Louvre. 23⅝ × 28⅝ in. (60 × 73 cm.). Painted with severely regular dense brush strokes rigidly organised into planes. It represents a local view near Aix, and was sold in 1894 for 170 francs.
Plate xxi	*Still life with soup tureen*, 1883–5. Paris, Louvre. 25½ × 32 in. (65 × 81.5 cm.). There is some doubt about the date of this painting. Both Douglas Cooper and Lawrence

XLII

XLIV

XLV

XL VI

XLVII

XLVIII

Gowing believe it to have been painted between 1875 and 1877, but Venturi, in his catalogue of Cézanne's works, has dated it 1883–5.

Plate xxii   *Jas de Bouffan*, 1882–5. Prague, National Gallery. 23¾ × 28¾ in. (60.5 × 73.5 cm.). This painting was sold to the National Gallery in Prague through Vollard, the art dealer. It is another view of Cézanne's house (see Plate xxiii). His studio was on the second floor, and he had another workshop on the ground floor. The house was sold by Cézanne in the late nineties, and paintings which he had done on the interior walls were destroyed.

Plate xxiii   *Trees at Jas de Bouffan*, c. 1885–7. London, The Courtauld Institute. 25½ × 31¼ in. (64.5 × 79 cm.). Jas de Bouffan – a thirty-seven-acre estate with a farm and an eighteenth-century house (see Plate xxii) on the outskirts of Aix-en-Provence – was inherited by Cézanne from his father. Cézanne made a number of paintings of the house as well as of the grounds. It played an important part in his life, as nowhere else did he work so often and so well.

Plate xxiv   *The blue vase*, 1885–7. Paris, Louvre. 24¼ × 20 in. (62 × 51 cm.). Cézanne produced a number of still-life paintings at this time, mostly in Aix.

Plate xxv   *Trees and houses*, 1885–7. New York, Lehman Collection. 26¾ × 36 in. (68 × 92 cm.). Bare trees creating a rhythmic pattern across a landscape – a frequent 'motif' of Cézanne's.

Plate xxvi   *Mount Sainte-Victoire*, c. 1886–8. London, The Courtauld Institute. 26 × 35⅜ in. (66 × 89.5 cm.). This is a subject which Cézanne drew and painted in oil and watercolour a number of times (see Plate xlvii).

Plate xxvii   *Aix: rocky landscape*, c. 1887. London, Tate Gallery. 25⅝ × 31⅞ in. (65 × 81 cm.). The Note to Plate xvii is applicable to this painting also, which is a good example of Cézanne's later simplification of form. The exact whereabouts of the scene of this painting is somewhat in doubt, some suggesting that the background of hills is situated at the end of the Chemin des Lauves (where Cézanne later had a studio). Douglas Cooper, however, maintains that the background strongly resembles the neighbourhood of Gardanne, a village south of Aix.

Plate xxviii   *Harlequin*, 1888–90. Cambridge, Lord Rothschild Collection. 36×25½ in. (91 ×64.5 cm.). This is an almost isolated treatment of the subject by Cézanne. As a painting it has had considerable influence on subsequent painters such as Picasso and Braque.

Plate xxix   *Still life with fruit basket*, 1888–90. Paris, Louvre. 25½×32 in. (65×81.5 cm.). This is a particularly rich example of Cézanne's power in still-life painting. Maurice Denis has said that what his contemporaries most admired in Cézanne's painting was the equilibrium, the simplicity, austerity and grandeur. His paintings seemed just as refined as, but more robust than, the strongest works of the Impressionists. 'Cézanne, by revealing structure beneath richly nuanced surfaces, went consciously beyond the appearances which satisfied a Monet.' Cézanne's famous remark that his aim was to 'vivify Poussin in contact with nature' is relevant here.

Plate xxx   *Pot of flowers and pears*, c. 1888–90. London, The Courtauld Institute. 17¾×21¼ in. (45×53.3 cm.).

Plate xxxi   *Portrait of Mme Cézanne in red*, c. 1890. Sao Paulo, Museum of Art. 35×27½ in. (89×70 cm.). This is a magnificent example of Cézanne's careful building of massive balance in an apparently simple, straightforward portrait. This portrait was painted soon after his marriage to Hortense Fiquet in 1886. The earlier portrait (Plate xiv) was painted before their marriage but after the birth of their son Paul.

Plate xxxii   *The card players*, c. 1892. London, The Courtauld Institute. 23½×28¾ in. (59.5 ×73 cm.). Cézanne painted five versions of this same subject at Aix during the early nineties. The model on the left is the same as in *Man smoking a pipe* (Plate xxxiii). These are important works in Cézanne's development.

Plate xxxiii   *Man smoking a pipe*, c. 1892. London, The Courtauld Institute. 28¾×23½ in. (73×59.5 cm.). Cézanne used this model in other paintings. He was a local gardener sometimes employed by Cézanne.

Plate xxxiv   *Still life with water jug*. c. 1892–3. London, Tate Gallery. 20⅞×28 in. (53×71 cm.). The blue water jug provides evidence that this was painted in Aix since it was found in Cézanne's last studio at the Chemin des Lauves. The jug also appears in other still lifes.

Plate xxxv   *Youth in a red waistcoat*, 1890–5. Private Collection. 36×29 in. (92×73 cm.). Said to have been painted from an Italian model whose name is supposed to have been Michelangelo da Rosa. There are three portraits of this model (see Plate xxxvi). This painting, when sold at a Sotheby auction in 1959, reached the price of £ 220,000. Cézanne has become a collector's painter of such importance that any example of his work to come under the hammer at this time is likely to command a comparable sum.

Plate xxxvi   *Youth in a red waistcoat*, 1890–5. Zurich, Bührle Collection. 31×25 in. (79×64 cm.). One of the most famous of Cézanne's late portraits. Geffroy wrote of this work, 'It can bear comparison with the finest figures in painting.' It contains so much of Cézanne's pictorial understanding that a study of it could provide one of the best introductions to his achievement.

Plate xxxvii   *Vase of tulips*, 1890–4. Chicago, The Art Institute. 23½×16⅝ in. (59.6×42.3 cm.).

Plate xxxviii   *Bathers*, 1890–4. Paris, Louvre. 8½×12½ in. (22×33 cm.). The use of short jabs of the brush, over and over again, one overlaying the other until he had finally resolved every inch of the canvas, is characteristic of Cézanne's late technique. The painting is created in great emotional intensity, being stabilised by the verticals in both background and figures. It was formerly in the collection of Maurice Denis.

Plate xxxix   *Still life with plaster cast*, c. 1895. Oil on paper on wood. London, The Courtauld Institute. 27½×22½ in. (69.5×57 cm.). The plaster cast is of a Cupid.

Plate xl   *Portrait of Joachim Gasquet*, 1896–7. Prague, National Gallery. 25⅝×21¼ in. (65.5×54.4 cm.). An unfinished portrait, particularly revealing of Cézanne's later method of thinly laid paint carefully, almost tentatively, covering the canvas. Gasquet, a poet and historian, was a very close friend of Cézanne's.

Plate xli   *The watchmaker*, c. 1895–1900. New York, Guggenheim Museum. 36½×28¾ in. (92.5×73.5 cm.). In the last years of his life, Cézanne had become something of a recluse, quarrelling even with his friends and admirers. Renoir, on one occasion, came to Aix to visit Cézanne, but, fearful of an unfriendly reception, left without calling on him. His models then were mainly local people who could be relied upon to remain silent and not to impose upon him.

Plate xlii *The lake of Annecy*, 1896. London, The Courtauld Institute. $25\frac{1}{2}\times32$ in. (64.5 $\times$81 cm.). Writing to Solari in 1896, from Talloires, near Annecy, Cézanne said, 'I miss Aix. Life for me is beginning to be of a sepulchral monotony . . . I paint to divert myself; it is not very amusing, but the lake is nice with the big mountains all round . . . It is not worth our country, though – without exaggeration – it is fine.'

Plate xliii *Old woman with rosary*, 1898–9. London, National Gallery. $31\frac{3}{4}\times25\frac{3}{4}$ in. (81$\times$ 65.5 cm.). The model is supposed to have been a woman who had left a convent and was employed in the Cézanne household as a servant. This, like *The watchmaker* (Plate xli) is an example of Cézanne's use of a model who might not be expected to impose on his reserve.

Plate xliv *Portrait of Ambroise Vollard*, 1899. Paris, Petit Palais Museum. $39\frac{1}{4}\times31\frac{1}{2}$ in. (100 $\times$81 cm.). Ambroise Vollard (1865–1939) was a famous Parisian art-dealer who, after dealing in the academic paintings of the day, in 1895 adopted Cézanne and arranged his first important exhibition – which was not a success. His gallery became one of the centres of Parisian art life during the early part of the century, and he has an important place in the development of modern art. Cézanne was a remarkably slow worker, and his care in the realisation of his understanding led to the remark, which he is quoted as having made of this painting: 'I am not displeased with the shirt front.'

Plate xlv *Still life with apples and oranges*, 1895–1900. Paris, Louvre. $28\frac{3}{4}\times36\frac{1}{4}$ in. (73 $\times$ 93 cm.).

Plate xlvi *Bathers*, 1898–1906. Philadelphia, Museum of Art. $82\times98\frac{1}{4}$ in. (208×249.5 cm.). This is the largest of the series of bathers which Cézanne painted late in life. Most of them were uncompleted at his death.

Plate xlvii *Mount Sainte-Victoire*, 1904. Philadelphia, Museum of Art. $27\frac{1}{2}\times35\frac{1}{4}$ in. (70 $\times$90 cm.).

Plate xlviii *The gardener*, c. 1906. London, Tate Gallery. $25\frac{3}{4}\times21\frac{5}{8}$ in. (65.5×55 cm.). This is a portrait of Cézanne's gardener and odd-job man Vallier. The painting was done in the garden outside Cézanne's studio in the Chemin des Lauves. It is one of his last works and is similar to one he was working on a few days before he died.